I0190132

Raising Godly Children in a Wicked World

by Jeffrey W. Hamilton

Raising Godly Children in a Wicked World by Jeffrey W. Hamilton

Copyright © 1996 by Jeffrey W. Hamilton. All rights reserved.

ISBN: 978-0-6151-7748-9

Table of Contents

Newborns

When Parents Learn Patience

Many changes come to a family when a child is born. New parents are usually unprepared for the differences in their lives, even with the best advanced warning. Even experienced parents experience shock when a new addition to the family arrives. With each child, I found myself remarking, "I had forgotten how trying a little one can be." Fortunately, there is more than enough joy and excitement with a newborn to make up for the difficult times. You see, with a newborn, it is the parents who have lessons to learn that will prepare them for raising children in the coming years.

We could discuss love, or devotion, or a number of other important topics, but the lesson parents need to learn the most is patience. Parents need patience to deal with the constant and untimely demands of the newborn child. It is not easy to have your sleep interrupted multiple times each night for months on end. A newborn is entirely dependent on you for everything, but he is unable to tell you exactly what is needed, except by the all inclusive word "WAAAAH!!" It may be disturbing to new parents to learn that this need for patience is not just a temporary phase. Parents need patience to deal with the tyrannical three-year-old trying to find the limits of his territory. Patience is also needed to comfort an ailing child when you feel like sobbing inside. It continues during the adolescent years when hormones sometimes make tempers flare over minor things. Does anyone doubt the need for patience when you teach your child how to drive, or when you are waiting up for your daughter to come back from her first big date?

Parents are forced to learn patience with a newborn. The newborn needs to be fed, changed, and played with. This would not be too difficult, but the demands a newborn makes come on the child's time schedule and not yours. It is hard to be loving and enthusiastic at 3 a.m., especially when the last demand was handled at 1 a.m. Time has no meaning to a newborn child. Playtime could happen at 2 in the morning just as easily as at 2 in the afternoon. It takes time to instruct a child who cannot be reasoned with that nights are for sleeping and days are for activities. It is this lack of communication that makes dealing with a newborn so frustrating. "Waaah!" (translated as "I'm hungry!") sounds strikingly similar to "Waaah!" (translated as "I'm lonely"). Parents soon develop a mental checklist . Does the diaper need changing? Perhaps he is hungry? Does he want to play or does he just want to be held? Misery is when you get to the bottom of your list and the answer is none of the above!

Every parent comes to the end of his or her wits at some point. We become frustrated at our inability to quiet the child. The important point is what do we do with our frustration. Some parents turn their frustration on themselves. "I'm a miserable parent. Why did I ever want a child? I must have been out of my mind!" Other parents turn their frustrations on their child. "Why can't you be happy!" If you think you are immune to this, remember that these frustrations come on new mothers while their hormones are settling back to their pre-pregnancy state. Postpartum blues are not a myth! The hormone changes frequently cause wild swings in emotions. Fathers are not immune either. The lack of sleep and constant irritating cries keep any parent from thinking clearly and logically. In weak moments, parents ascribe motives to their newborn that cannot exist: "You're just doing this to annoy me" or "You only scream when we sit down to eat. You're trying to keep me from enjoying a meal."

Therefore, every parent needs to learn patience. In I Thessalonians 5:14, we learn that we must be patient with everyone, that includes our own children. Our family is not an exception to the rule. Trials brings about patience through the testing of our faith (James 1:2-4). We often think about this verse in terms of religious persecution, but believe me when I say that handling the demands of a newborn is a trial; sitting up late in the night with a sick child is a trial; waiting for your daughter to get back from her first date is a trail. These trials test our faith. Can we really depend on God's help or do we think we should be able to handle our problems by ourselves? Can we turn to God in prayer and trust God's answer to our pleas? These trials discipline us and train us, but no discipline is fun to endure (Hebrews 12:11). However, in the end, we learn the lesson of peace.

Look at how Peter describes the effects of suffering in I Peter 5:10. Suffering perfects us - in other words, it brings us to maturity. Suffering establishes us - in other words, it plants us firmly in our beliefs. It strengthens us - in other words, suffering helps us to endure whatever comes next in our life. Finally, it settles us - in other words, it makes us level-headed. There is nothing like raising a child to mold two newly married youngsters into level-headed adults. Peter's thoughts read much like Paul's description of older men, who are to be temperate, dignified, sensible, sound in faith, in love, and in perseverance.

Patience is not a natural trait. Some of us start out with more patience than others, but we all must bring our patience to full maturity. Patience is a by-product of following the will of God (Galatians 5:22-23). In all the fruits of the Spirit are characteristics that every Christian parent needs to properly raise godly children. Remember that a servant of God must be gentle to all, able to teach, patient (II Timothy 2:24).

Training a newborn takes patience. "Training, what training?" you may ask. Even with a newborn, there are many lessons to teach. Newborns need to learn the difference between night and day. Every new parent is eager to have their child learn this lesson as quickly as possible. Some children get the hang of it quickly, others may take months or even years to learn to sleep through the night. Our children tended to take 10 months to a year to reach that point. We struggled with envy every time someone would say, "Oh, our Joey slept through the night a week after we got home from the hospital." Take heart, it eventually happens. I suspect a large portion of the problem is a child most grow enough to be able to store enough food to last through the night; we tended to have small children. How do you train a child to sleep at night? Establish patterns or rituals that signal the coming of bedtime. Even adults have difficulty going from full-steam to deep-sleep without some time to slow down and prepare for bed. End each day by reading a story or singing a song. Both of these bedtime rituals will have benefits for your child as they grow older. Have the last feeding in a dim room to signal the end of a day. Also, try to give the child a fixed place to sleep. If you have to do some traveling, bring the child's crib blanket or other items he sleeps with. A child finds the familiar comfortable.

A child also needs to learn that Mom and Dad are loving and dependable. Cries are not ignored forever. This doesn't mean that every time a newborn whimpers, that a parent must drop everything, but no child should be left crying for a long time. Sometimes a child must be left to cry for a little while. A baby must be put down while Mom gets dinner ready, even if the child would much rather play. Even with the best habits, a child will not always be ready to go to sleep at bedtime. Sometimes, when all else fails, you will have to allow a child to cry himself to sleep. These times are very hard on a parent's nerves. There is nothing more grating on the nerves than a small child's cry, especially when it is your baby. However, the child is learning that every problem isn't solved immediately, though problems are eventually worked out. One "trick" that my wife and I learned was to lay our wound-up child down at bedtime and allow him to cry. Eventually, he would start to get tired of crying (even a baby can't go on forever -- even though it seems like it at the time!). You can tell when they get tired by the change in their cry. At that time, one of us would go into the child's room and comfort him until he stopped crying and started to go to sleep. We would then lay the child down. Often this ritual would have to be repeated two, three, or four times in a row, but eventually he would fall asleep. Soon, the child would protest, but would quickly go to sleep just by putting him in bed. The surest way to ruin this training is to give in to the crying and take the child out to play with him. Then he will quickly learn to get his own way just by outlasting his parents.

As I mentioned before, patience doesn't end here. You will need patience while dealing with your children throughout their lives. You need patience to deal with the endless questions a preschooler comes up with. You also need patience to deal with a child's stubbornness, his flights of fancy, or his pleadings for just one more piece of candy. It is easy to forget that it takes time for any lesson to be learned. Writing may come easily to you, but for a little one writing is a major chore. I can easily write a four or five page typed letter in a few hours in the evening, yet I still remember the trauma of writing a ten page report on Scotland in the fifth grade. "Ten pages! How can anyone write ten pages on one subject!" It took me over a month to write that report. Just because a task is easy for you, doesn't mean that the same skill is inbred in your child. My wife constantly wonders why our boys can't be neat -- she was always a tidy person, even when she was young. I just smile and say they take after their Dad. I can't do anything without making a large mess, though I have learned to clean up after myself (well, most of the time).

No child remains a newborn forever. This stage will pass and you will move on to other things and other problems. It may seem odd, but there will be times when you wish they were small once more, when you could hold them in your arms and cuddle them while they were sleeping. For every grief that a newborn gives a parent, God has balanced it with many, many joys and precious moments. Concentrate on these simple pleasures and the trials will move on quickly -- too quickly.

Changing Attitudes

Age 4: "My parents can do anything."
Age 8: "There might be one or two things they don't know."
Age 12: "Naturally, my parents don't understand."
Age 14: "I never realized how hopelessly old fashioned they are."
Age 21: "You would expect them to feel that way; they are out of date."
Age 25: "They come up with a good idea now and then."
Age 30: "I wonder what Mom and Dad think I should do?"
Age 40: "Let's be patient until we discuss it with our parents."
Age 50: "What would Mom and Dad have thought about it?"
Age 60: "I wish I could talk it over with them one more time."

Author Unknown

Little Eyes Upon You

There are little eyes upon you and they're watching night and day.
There are little ears that quickly take in every word you say.
There are little hands all eager to do anything you do;
And a little boy who's dreaming of the day he'll be like you.

You're the little fellow's idol, you're the wisest of the wise.
In his little mind about you no suspicions ever rise.
He believes in you devoutly, holds all you say and do;
He will say and do, in your way when he's grown up just like you.

There's a wide-eyed little fellow who believes you're always right;
And his eyes are always opened, and he watches day and night.
You are setting an example every day in all you do;
For the little boy who's waiting to grow up to be like you.

Author Unknown

Toddlers

Giving Love and Security

Around nine months to two years of age, children move into the toddler phase of development. It is a wonderful time. Everything is a new and fresh delight to the child. The world has never been experienced and everything has to be pushed, poked and tasted to see how it reacts. This curiosity often concerns parents because toddlers get into **everything**! The playing with forbidden things is not due to maliciousness, but a simple curiosity at what is behind the object or what happens when an object is manipulated.

During the toddler phase, children begin to communicate and parents begin to breathe a sigh of relief. Now you have a clue as to what a child needs or wants, even if it is only a grunt accompanied by a pudgy hand pointing at the refrigerator. Pronunciation at this age is innovated, which leaves parents often guessing what "tvif" means. Visitors to the home are usually left without a clue. Little do they know that parents with multiple children will often call an older child in to translate for them. Another interesting problem is the toddler's vocabulary is so small that one word is used for everything. A toddler learns to call his father "Dah," but Mom is dismayed to find out that she is "Dah" along with every other adult in the world. Fortunately, this passes. However, a parent must be careful not to misinterpret an overused word. "No" may not mean defiance. He could be saying, "Not now" or "Not that color" or "Not that way" or "This tastes odd" or "I can't eat, I have to get to the bathroom" or any number of other things.

An important lesson that parents can teach their toddlers is the concept of love. You can't set a toddler, who can't even pronounce the word "milk", down and give a discourse on love. Love is best taught by example. We can learn how to give and teach love by learning from our own heavenly Father. Our children learn about God by observing us. In a sense, we are a tangible representation of God to our children.

Our Father's love is secure (Romans 8:35-39). There is nothing that can separate us from God's love. God has shown the firmness of His love when He sent His son into a world that had rejected Him to rescue the world from their own sins. As a result, we are secure in our knowledge of God's love for us. It also makes us secure in general, knowing the extent that God has gone to keep us safe. Our love to our children should be of the same sort. Few of us will ever be called upon to die for our children, but we can show the firm commitment of our love for them, even when they are being bad. Every child needs this security so they can face the world with confidence.

Love does not translate into spoiling a child. Our heavenly Father gives us what we need, not the things we think we want (Matthew 7:9-11). Spoiling a child is not in the child's best interest. If we give a child everything he wants, he learns "I am, therefore I get." Such a child is not prepared for life in the real world. Parents need to focus on giving things that will benefit a child. Even if you can afford many "extras" for your child, you should refrain from giving them to your children. The little "extras" should only be given if you can articulate how having the "extra" will improve the child. Not getting everything you want is a very important lesson and a difficult one for many parents to teach.

A mother's love for her child must be so strong that she is willing to give up her child to protect him. Fortunately, few mothers have to test their love to this extent, but look at the examples in the Scriptures. Moses' mother placed her son in a basket in a river to keep the Egyptians from killing him (Exodus 2:3). God rewarded her love by saving Moses and allowing his own mother to raise him through childhood. Samuel's mother wanted a child so much that when God granted her a child, she was willing to send him to the tabernacle after he was weaned to be raised by the priests (I Samuel 2:19). God rewarded her love by giving her other children, but can you imagine willingly devoting your firstborn to God and only seeing him once a year? Think about the mother who appeared before Solomon (I Kings 3:26). We often talk about Solomon's wisdom in determining who was the true mother, but think about the mother's love. She was willing to let the woman who stole her child raise him up rather than to see him killed. Truly a mother's love is a powerful and enduring love (Isaiah 49:15). While many women have no difficulties showing such love, we must not assume that it is instinctive. A mother's love is taught (Titus 2:4). It is often passed down from mother to daughter, but it can also be learned from other women who have tread life's pathway ahead of you.

Many new parents wonder when they should start teaching their children. Teaching starts the day a child is born, but it begins to get serious now that a child is a toddler. Proverbs 22:6 tells us that if we train a child while he is young, righteous actions will become a habit when they are older. We need to instill good habits in our youngsters. To get good habits, we have to set good examples. You can't expect a child to understand the subtleties of "do what I say, not what I do." What kind of habits am I talking about? Children need to have bedtime habits: brushing their teeth, reading a Bible story, and saying a prayer. Continued application of these habits will benefit them physically and spiritually through the rest of their lives. We can also instill good attitudes by teaching good morning habits. Now I know some of us are total grouches in the morning, at least until we have had our coffee, but is that a good habit to instill in a child? I know a mother who waits until she hears her child stirring and then walks into the room with a bright sunny smile and a cheerful "Good Morning!" even when she doesn't feel like it. Oh, so subtly, she is teaching her child to start each day with a fresh, happy attitude and to be thankful to God for another day to do His will. Don't you wish we all had that habit? We can also teach toddlers good eating habits. They learn that meals come at certain times and that snacks, though they taste wonderful, are limited. Even though these are eating habits, they teach spiritual lessons as well -- you can't have everything right when you want it or every time you want it. You can also encourage good eating by treating good foods, such as fruit and vegetables, as special snacks. When a child wants a snack, offer a choice between an apple, orange, or carrot sticks and try not to look shocked when a child picks a carrot stick once in a while.

Parents need to teach their toddlers that there are limits to what they can do. Oddly enough, having limits gives a child security. Even grownups need limits. The most difficult decisions are those that present too many choices, but limit those choices to two or three things and most people have little difficulty in picking one. Children need to know where the limits are to feel comfortable and secure. Enforcing the limits with a toddler is not hard. Light spankings and scoldings are often very effective in letting a child know that something is off limits. However, don't be deceived in thinking that these things will always stop a child. Curiosity is strong in a toddler and they will want to find out what happens if they disobey Mom or Dad. Frequently, parents find themselves repeating the discipline over and over and over again. It is not unusual to wonder if there isn't something wrong in the mental processes of the child. How many times does it take for it to sink into a child's mind that you are not going to let them touch the hot pot on the stove? Remember our first lesson. Here is an opportunity to practice all that patience you learned earlier. It is extremely important that children learn as soon as possible that listening to parents is important for their own well-being (Proverbs 1:33). Once in a while a parent should let a child find out the hard way that disobeying them is not a good idea. The events should be carefully picked as not being harmful to the child and they should be well-warned what will happen if they don't listen, but if they persist, let them learn that what Mom or Dad said is true. For example, if you just mopped the kitchen floor and you tell the tot not to run through the kitchen because they might fall, sometimes it helps that when he makes a dash through the middle of the floor (where he won't bang his head on a sharp corner) to hold your peace while he tries out the padding on his bottom side. Then you can move in, comfort the child, and say, "See, Mommy told you, you might fall. You need to listen to Mommy." These natural consequences to wrongful actions are often powerful lessons. Despite our best precaution, toddlers will hurt themselves. Comfort the child, but don't pass up the opportunity to point out that it happened because they didn't listen.

Disciplining toddlers takes a lot of repetition, which means parents will have to be consistent. Consistency is what gives Christians security. They know that God always remains the same (Hebrews 13:8; Psalms 62:1-2). A child needs to know that something isn't off-limit just because you are having a bad day or you are too rushed to watch over the child. If something is wrong, it must remain wrong. This is going to make a good bit of work for busy parents because they are going to have to be watchful that the rules are being followed.

Training in the Scriptures can begin with a toddler. You don't need sit-down lectures to learn biblical lessons (Deuteronomy 6:7). We teach our children first and foremost by living a righteous life with them. By showing our trust in God and His wisdom, we teach our children security for their whole life (Proverbs 3:19-26). Keep the lessons simple for toddlers. Teach "God is love" by showing the toddler Mom and Dad's love for him. Show him that "God is good" through the kindness that Mom and Dad shows him. Encourage him to share his things. Most, though not all, toddlers tend to share their things. Just last night, a toddler offered me a piece of chewed bread stick. Even if you don't like what is offered, encourage the gesture with profuse thanks. Toddlers also tend to be natural helpers. Often they return things they find laying around the house, even the decorative items from the coffee table. Although it is sometimes annoying to have all this "help," the good trait of helping needs to be encouraged. Always keep the child's viewpoint in mind. "Helping Mommy" or exploring the back reaches of the kitchen cabinet may be an irritant to you, but we must be careful we don't teach the wrong lesson because we are annoyed.

As with each topic that we explore, the teaching of love and security doesn't stop when a children grows beyond being a toddler. The ideas remain the same, the principles remain consistent, just the application varies as our children grow.

Blurred Barriers

I've never studied all the rules
      'Bout curbs and discipline,
But I can't buy the idea
      You're training children when
You let them tear the schoolhouse down
      And still leave them alone.
The finest colt is worthless 'til
      You put the bridle on!

Revoking laws won't make a crook
      Become an honest man.
Removing railings from a curve
      Won't make it safer and
If cows are prone to jump the fence
      Removing it may stop
Fence-jumping problems but it won't
      Do much to save your crop.

Author Unknown

Two and Three-Year-Olds

Limits Tested

What parent hasn't been warned about the terrible twos and threes? What causes the dread? By the time a child reaches the age of two or three, he is no longer completely dependent on his parents. Two and three-year-olds can efficiently move about. They can run, climb, and manipulate objects, but they haven't learned how to do any of these things safely. Two and three-year-olds can now express their desires, but they haven't learned tact. They now have a measure of independence, but they have no restraint.

Surely this is a trying time for parents. The once passive child now demands that things be done his way. The cereal must be served in the green bowl. When Dad gets home, junior wants him to play now, not later. Supper must be familiar items. I sometimes believe my children at this age could live off peanut butter and jelly three meals a day, seven days a week. Meanwhile, the poor parent is thinking, "What kind of monster have I brought into this world?" or "There must have been some mix up at the hospital, surely this can't be one of mine!" or "Where did I lose that sweet child of only a few months ago?"

Have you ever awaked at night in an unfamiliar, dark room? Moving about is difficult and sometimes painful. Most of us make timid, careful steps to the light switch. Once the lights are on and you can see the placement of the walls and furniture, movement becomes vastly easier. All people need to know where the limits are to be secure -- children are no exception. Have you ever noticed that young children will often cling to their parents, especially in unfamiliar surroundings? They will make brief forays away from their parents, but they will always run back for a little time with Mom. It can be annoying when you are trying to get supper on the table. However, the children need to know you are there and available when they need you.

We live our whole life with rules and restrictions. No one can avoid them. A child being raised in this world needs to be trained to respect authority and to follow the rules (Proverbs 22:6). Even adults have to learn to live with restrictions. Paul tells us in I Corinthians 6:12 that every lawful thing is not always helpful to a person. Later, in I Corinthians 10:23, Paul says that everything that exists doesn't necessarily build a person up. We learn the rules and live with the restrictions.

Two and three-year-olds will test your limits on their behavior. Where is the line? Is it firm? Does "no" really mean no? To survive this period, parents must have a firm idea about exactly what is acceptable and unacceptable behavior. It also means parents must be prepared to enforce the rules. Solomon said that rest and delight from a child only comes after diligent effort to correct his behavior (Proverbs 29:17).

The Bible has much to say about disciplining children. Our love for our children requires that we discipline them (Proverbs 13:24). Our heavenly Father is our best example (Hebrews 12:3-11). Disciplining is not fun for the child or for the parent, but it is essential for the development of character. When a child is not disciplined, we are showing the world that we do not care about the welfare of the child. Discipline removes the foolishness or silliness from a child (Proverbs 22:15). Young children do not understand the need to limit their actions. They don't understand that standing on their toes on a rocking chair means their head is likely to contact the corner of the coffee table. Children need to be disciplined to learn they cannot do what they want, when they want.

Some parents are afraid to spank their children. A lot of junk psychology exists that claims spanking is a form of child abuse. Abused children suffer psychological damage, so it is assumed that spanking causes damage to the child's personality. The creator of all humans has a different opinion. Spanking a child, when properly done, will NOT harm a child (Proverbs 23:13-14). It is actually critical to a child's spiritual development. Spanking teaches wisdom to a child and prevents embarrassment in the future (Proverbs 29:15). If you don't believe me, think about those screaming kids in the stores and restaurant who are demanding things. Would you like to be in his mother's place? Yet, she brought it upon herself by not setting and enforcing limits on her child's behavior.

All these passages talk about the use of a "rod." A rod is a branch or scion, a slender stick or, in more modern terms, a switch. You can see this definition in passages such as Jeremiah 1:11 and Genesis 30:37. A proper switch is a slim, flexible branch off a tree or a bush. A switch applied to the buttocks stings fiercely. It may leave red marks or bruises, but it causes no lasting damage. I have noticed that most men manage to get by spanking with their hand, but children don't seem to be affected by many women's hand spanking. A switch equalizes the application of discipline. However, even men should consider using a switch, even if they can effectively spank with their hand. To use a switch requires at least a small amount of consideration. You have to go and get a switch. The extra time can give you a chance to consider exactly why you are punishing the child and how much discipline needs to be given.

15

It is important to know when you need to discipline a child, especially with a two or three-year-old. First, make sure that the child is listening to you and understands what you are saying. Small children are easily distracted and they may not hear you, even if they are physically in your presence. Have the child look you in the eyes while you are talking to him and ask him to acknowledge that he heard you. Some families still insist their children say "Yes, ma'am" or "Yes, sir" when they are told something. This is not just old fashion politeness. It is a way to ensure that you are not talking to a brick wall. Make sure that you phrase your rules in terms that a two or three-year-old can understand. You need to use simple words and concepts. "It's bedtime. Pick up your toys," is straight forward. "Honey, go out to the garage and get Daddy's phillips-head screwdriver out of the toolbox on the second shelf," is woefully inadequate. Few two or three-year-olds can grasp more than one idea at a time. Avoid giving children at this age instructions that consist of a series of steps. Give them one step and when it is completed, instruct them in the next step.

Punish a two or three-year-old who willfully disobeys instruction or does not complete a request due to negligence. I am not talking about accidents. Few parents permit their children to dump a glass of milk on the carpet, but glasses turn over on the best of us. If a child is told not to reach across the table, but he does anyway and knocks over his milk in the process, then a punishment should be administered. Often, you can see the willfulness in a child's eyes. Every parent of a two or three-year-old has seen the "I dare you" look in a child's eye. I have seen three-years-olds get their parent's attention before they proceed to break a rule. You may be thinking, "What is this child doing?" What he is doing is testing the limits. It is an outgrowth of that natural curiosity you saw when he was one. He wants to know where the limits are and are you always willing to enforce them.

Punishment should always be due to a child breaking a rule. Never punish a child because you had a bad day at the office or because Junior kept you up half the night with a cold. However, don't forego punishing an infraction because you had a bad day, either. The punishment should be consistent with the violation, not with the mood of the parent. Which leads to the question, "How much punishment is appropriate?"

Punishment is not punishment unless it hurts in some way. A spanking should be just severe enough to make the child to not want to repeat the wrongful behavior. The use of a switch on the bottom or back thighs will not cause permanent injuries (Proverbs 23:13-14). It may leave red marks or bruises, but they will heal, along with the spiritual problem (Proverbs 20:30). Solomon says that parents should chasten (literally "blows"), while there is hope of turning your child from destruction (Proverbs 19:18). Too many parents put off training their children. The easiest time to train a child is when he is young. If you wait too long, the child may have gone too far down the path of destruction to rescue.

Do not misinterpret these passages to mean that God is advocating child abuse. When a child is two or three, start with a single swat with a switch. The startlement alone is sufficient punishment at the beginning. If the child quickly repeats the wrong action, then a single swat wasn't enough, so punish the second infraction with two blows. If he does it again, use four blows. It may take repeated application as the child presses to find out if "no" really means "no" all the time. Eventually, the child will give in. If you give in first, the child quickly learns that you have your limits. If they want something bad enough, all they have to do is endure a bit of pain for a while and they can get what they want. If you haven't been punishing your children, when you do start, you may be surprised how many wacks it takes to get a strong-willed child to mind. Remind yourself that you are making up for lost time and that soon it won't take as many blows. Often, simply going to get the switch corrects the problem. However, in those cases, a wack or two should still be given or a child won't mind unless you have a switch in your hand. As a child grows older, you will have to increase the initial number of wacks. If you find the switching is not effective on an older child, apply them to their bare bottom. Fortunately, consistent spanking leads to less spanking as a child grows older (Proverbs 22:6).

Keep the punishment between you and the child. Take him off to the side where his friends and siblings cannot gloat over his punishment. Punishing a child in front of other children just encourages the other children to tattle on the child to see him get in trouble. Never, ever, let another child deliver a punishment for you. Every child should learn that punishment is the exclusive right of a parent.

When you are dealing with a two or three-year-old, you must punish wrongful action at the time of the infraction. A two-year-old will not associate a punishment "when Daddy gets home" with a misdeed that morning. Two and three-year-olds live in the now. They have yet to develop the concepts of past and future. This is why you often repeat yourself. Johnny learned last week that he could not have a cookie just before dinner, and here he is trying to sneak one again this week. They may remember last week's punishment but they don't associate it with this week's desire.

Be careful not to accidentally reward defiance. Do not give in to a child's desire just because little Johnny is more stubborn than you are. Also, don't give in just because it is not a convenient time -- such as being at a store or in a restaurant. If you permit misbehavior when others are around, then a child learns to wait until there is an audience to defy you. Unfortunately, in many areas, modern zealots will misinterpret your punishment of misbehavior as child abuse. It is important for you to be willing to obey God instead of living in fear of what men may do to you. Just be confident that God will care for you, if you follow His directions.

There are many things that you can teach your two and three-year-olds about God. They can learn reverence for God and Jesus by learning to be quiet in worship and classes. They learn respect for authority by learning to obey Mom and Dad's rules. They learn about sharing when they can't always get the toy that they want. You can teach them the concept of prayer by allowing them to "say a prayer" after Dad gives thanks for the food. They can learn that certain actions are wrong, such as lying, stealing or disobeying.

Introduce the major characters of the Bible to the child by using simple themes. Talk about Adam and Eve to discuss the need to do what God said. The story of Cain and Abel can be used to discuss caring for others. Abraham is a great example about trusting God. Joseph, Moses, and Daniel can all be used to talk about God's protection. God's love is shown through Jesus. Children of this age can also learn some of the major events in the Bible, such as the Creation and the Flood.

Four and Five-Year-Olds

Obedience Training

Preschoolers (and kindergartners) can communicate in complex ways. They become an endless source of "Why?" It is no longer enough to know that something exists. They want a reason for it. They are not asking "Why?" to get a detailed explanation, but to see the logic and order in this world. Perhaps you will be asked, "Why is the sky blue?" You could give a detailed scientific explanation that would make your physics teacher proud. However, the child will probably be lost before the first sentence is completed. A better answer may be to say that when light shines through things, it sometimes picks up a color. Get a colored glass and shine a flashlight through it. Then say that air gives light a blue color when the sun shines through it. Is it absolutely accurate? No, but it is good enough for a four-year-old. "Why?" is a four-year-old's way of engaging in grownup talk with Mom and Dad. Sometimes they are not interested in the actual answer so much as to be able to say something and have Mom or Dad respond to them.

Naturally, with all this questioning going on, you can expect your rules to be questioned. "Why can't I stay up late?" "Why do I have to go to bed?" "Why do I have to take a bath?" Give a simple, reasonable answer if you feel it is appropriate, but remember you don't have to justify your decisions. If your five-year-old doesn't like the answer, an "I'm sorry you don't agree, but that is the way it is in my house" is a good answer. Both children and parents want appreciation, so when a parent's authority is questioned we sometimes doubt ourselves -- even when the questions come from a preschooler. Remember who is the parent and who is the child. Children need to learn obedience even when they don't understand all the reasons. Isn't this what God expects of His children? Sometimes a "because God said so" has to be good enough. A child needs to learn that "because Mom said so" has to be good enough as well.

As your child develops, he is building on things that he already knows. His movement improves, his speech improves, and his vocabulary improves. The growth around the ages of four and five is very noticeable. A lot of the change comes from the loss of baby fat as his activity increases. A child's memory also develops at this age. For many of us, our earliest recollections come from this period. With the memory comes a sense of time, which leads to a new set of woes. "Dad, when are we going to get there?!!!?"

Just because you have established the limits, it doesn't follow that they are regularly followed. Children sometimes break rules through carelessness. They are easily distracted and forget to be careful with the rules. Sometimes a child just becomes plain lazy about doing what he is told; after all, there are many things that he would rather be doing that are more interesting. And then there is the dreaded rebellious child who doesn't like being told what to do.

Parents need to concentrate on teaching obedience. Rules must be followed whether Mom or Dad is standing over the children or not. In Ephesians 6:4, Paul said that it is right for a child to obey his parents. In Colossians 3:20, Paul said that obedience is pleasing to God. When a child listens to his Dad and Mom, his obedience will make him look good (Proverbs 1:8-9). It is a sign of the decay of this age when men are disobedient to their parents (II Timothy 3:2).

Obedience cannot occur unless the rules are enforced. The primary means of enforcement is spanking as we discussed in the previous chapter. For each misdeed, there must be a just recompense (Hebrews 2:2-3). Spanking should not be done because we are personally insulted by a child's disobedience, but to teach our children to honor authority. The best time to teach obedience is when you can control the environment. For example, your children need to know that they cannot play with some things. Don't wait until you are in a store to teach your children not to touch crystal on the shelf. When your child first begins to crawl and reaches for something he shouldn't have, our first instinct as a parent is to move the item out of his reach. A valuable opportunity for learning is lost when we do this. Instead, move the item within his reach and keep a small switch in your hand. When he starts to grab the object, tell him "No" in a quiet voice and move his hand away. When he reaches for the object again, tell him "No" again in a quiet voice and switch the back of his hand. It usually only takes a few times before the child decides there are better things to do with his time. Even better for the parent is that the training remains. You can tell a child that something is "No" and expect the item not to be touched. Of course, you have to be consistent. One slip of letting a child touch something after telling him "No" will defeat months' worth of training.

You can also teach a child obedience by letting the consequences of his actions be the punishment. Christ learned obedience through His suffering (Hebrews 5:8). It is hard to think of the creator of this world learning obedience, yet it happened because God let Him suffer. Often, we are too protective of our children. We don't let them suffer the consequences of their actions. One gentleman told me that he was afraid that his children would fall into a nearby pond when his wife and he were not looking. When the children were just toddlers, he let them wonder over to the pond while he walked behind them. As children are wont to do, they eventually fell into the water. He let them thrash just long enough to realize they were in trouble, but not long enough to swallow the pond and he pulled them out. He said they never wandered near the pond again until he took them there to teach them to swim.

Simply following the rules is not enough, we must also teach our children to gladly obey. God expects His children to follow him with all of their heart (Deuteronomy 26:16). We can't be pleasing to God if we drag our feet and say, "Aww, do we have too???" Most parents accidentally teach their children reluctant obedience. How many of us have grumbled about having to go to work or to church? Is it surprising then for a child to grumble about having to go to school? Parents also encourage their children to complain. When your child says he doesn't like what you fixed for dinner, do you make them something else? You just rewarded your child for complaining! I can't count the number of parents I have seen encourage their child to delay obedience. "Johnny, pick up that toy....Did you hear me, I said pick up that toy!...If you don't pick up that toy right NOW, I'm going to have to do something drastic!...That does it young man, I'm going to swat your little bottom." Usually, Johnny then quickly picks up the toy, smiles sweetly to his Mom, who forgets all about the threatened spanking. She pats herself on the back for making Johnny be obedient, but she doesn't realize what else she has taught him. Johnny has learned that he doesn't have to do what Mom says until she goes to get the switch. Not only that, but if he smiles sweetly, he can avoid the spanking. Invest the time to teach your children to obey you immediately. Delays should be answered with a quiet rebuke and a spanking, not threats.

Some parents don't discourage their children from whining or talking back. Direct punishment will stop the outward disagreement, but sometimes we can do a bit more to insure that obedience is done willingly. Make sure that the consequences of whining are less favorable than quiet obedience. If they whine about leaving their game to come eat supper, send them to their room while the rest eat and allow them to have their meal after everyone else is done. I had one child who complained about having to eat a vegetable his Mom had prepared. Without saying a word, I doubled the portion on his plate. "You don't expect me to eat all of it, do you?!" I quietly added another spoonful. "Mom!" My wife just gave him a puzzled look and said, "Haven't you figured out that you are going to eat more for each complaint?" It took him a long time to finish dinner that night, but he ate every bite. His frequent complaints also stopped. Another option is if a child states they don't like dinner, give them the option of skipping dinner. Of course, there will not be anything else available to eat until breakfast. This is not a punishment, but their choice. Growing children quickly decide that any food is better than going hungry. If you have a child who continually is late for dinner, simply make it a rule that if they are not there, they don't get to eat until the next meal time.

And then there is the "I didn't hear you" syndrome. Sometimes it is legitimate. Mom yells from the kitchen that dinner is ready and the kids are so engrossed in the latest action video downstairs that they did not notice her call. Make sure your children hear you. Don't teach them to tune you out at their convenience. When talking to them, place your hand on their shoulder. Make them look you in the eye as you talk to them. This way, you know you have their undivided attention. If what you are asking them to do is complex, have them repeat your instructions. If you call them from another room, require them to give a response to indicate they heard you. The old fashion "Yes, sir" and "Yes, ma'am" is not just politeness, they give parents responses that the child was listening. If you don't get a response, don't yell again. Immediately go and correct the inattentiveness. Don't establish a habit in your child by saying things that they can safely ignore.

Learning to listen is an important life skill. We should not let it slide by. Make your children wait for you to finish talking before they dash off to do what you say. "Sara, will you get my Bible? It's on the kitchen table." Meanwhile, Sara is already out the door by the time you said the word "get." Soon she returns and says "I can't find it." Don't go and get it yourself. Ask the child where you told her to find the Bible. You know she wasn't listening, but this makes her understand what the problem was. If you give in and get the Bible yourself, you teach the child that not paying attention means you can get out of a chore quickly.

Children also need to learn not to color the things they hear with what they would like to hear. "Can I have a cookie?" "You can have one after dinner." You soon turn around and find a cookie in his hand. And his explanation? "You said I could have one." Or there is the multiplying cookie trick. "Can I have a cookie?" "Just one" and Junior walks off with one in each hand and one in his mouth. Children and grownups are often guilty of hearing what they want to hear instead of what is actually said. Make sure you teach them to listen attentively and accurately.

Another common problem is the "I forgot" syndrome. You ask a child to pick up his toys and ten minutes later you find him outside on the tricycle. "Did you get all the toys picked up?" "Oh, I forgot," as he dashes back into the house. As Christians, God expects us to remember His laws by doing those laws (James 1:25). Children, too, can only learn the house rules by doing them. Initially, you will have to teach your child to remember by periodically checking on them. Too many parents tell a child to do something and then never check to see if it is done until it is too late. Do you tell a small child to get dressed for church and then get angry when you start to walk out the door and find they are still in their pajamas? Parents have to teach remembrance to their children by periodically checking on them. At first, you will have to look in on them every few minutes. If they are not following instructions, discipline them with a switch. As they learn to concentrate on the task at hand, start to stretch out the times you check on them. Your goal is for them to do something to completion without you having to stand over them.

Be careful not to accidentally teach your children only to work when you are coming to check on them. Some children wait until they hear Mom's footsteps in the hall to "remember" to clean their room. A child like that will grow up to goof off at work when the boss isn't looking. Rebuke a child who takes far longer than is reasonable to accomplish a task. However, make sure your idea of a reasonable length of time is reasonable for the child's abilities.

Somewhere along the line, every child tries yelling and screaming to get what he wants. If a parent gives in to the demands just once, they will be subject to repeated episodes. A tantrum should be an automatic denial of whatever the child is demanding. If they want a cookie, they should be calmly told that for their outburst they don't get any deserts for the rest of the day. If they are wanting attention, send them to their room after switching them for their misbehavior. Many modern psychologist claim that spanking a child who is having a tantrum does not help or causes some future problem. This is absolute nonsense. No child continues actions that result in their own discomfort -- especially when it is accompanied by a denial of their demands.

Be careful not to reward a child's partial obedience. God expects His children to do all that He commands (Joshua 1:8). Suppose you tell Johnny to pick up his room before bedtime. Johnny manages to get two items put away while playing the next hour. Now what do you do? If you keep him up until he finishes picking up his room, he has learned that partial obedience lets you stay up late. If you tell him to finish it in the morning, he has learned that partial obedience lets you get out of a task, at least for the moment, giving you more time to play. Instead, a parent needs to give the child a reasonable amount of time to complete the task. Don't have them start to pick up their room five minutes before bedtime. There is no way they can complete the task and you will encourage them to only partially obey your instructions. If you forget to tell them in time, then it is your problem. Wait until the next morning when there is sufficient time. Don't make your forgetfulness a cause for teaching partial obedience. Check on their progress while there is a reasonable amount of time to correct their goofing off.

Obedience training applies to our children's time in church. Now is the time to teach them to sit still in class and worship services. Sitting still is a part of a person's listening skills and it is needed for worship and school. Children need to be encouraged to participate in class and in worship. They can answer questions, bow their heads in prayer, and join with the brethren in singing praise to our God. Encourage your children to memorize simple verses or parts of verses each week. Teach them songs. Help them learn the books of the Bible.

> To educate a child in mind and not in morals is to educate a menace to society.
>
> Woodrow Wilson

Thoughts for Now and Later

Some day when my children are old enough to understand the logic that motivates a mother, I will tell them:

"I loved you enough to ask where you were going, with whom, and what time you would be home.

I loved you enough to insist that you save your money and buy a bike for yourself even though we could afford to buy one for you.

I loved you enough to be silent and let you discover that your new best friend was a creep.

I loved you enough to make you take a Milky Way back to the drugstore (with a bite out of it) and tell the clerk, 'I stole this yesterday and want to pay for it.'

I loved you enough to stand over you for two hours while you cleaned your room, a job that would have taken me five minutes.

I loved you enough to let you see anger, disappointment, and tears in my eyes. Children must learn that their parents are not perfect.

I loved you enough to let you assume the responsibility for your actions even when the penalties were so harsh they almost broke my heart.

But most of all, I loved you enough to say 'No' when I knew you would hate me for it. Those were the most difficult battles of all. I am glad I won them, because in the end, you won something too."

Mother

Five to Nine-Year-Olds

Responsibility Training

It is amazing how quickly our children grow. The years just fly by with wild abandon. Somewhere between the age of five and six, our children begin their formal schooling. The children have been learning up to this point. They have learned to talk, walk, dress and feed themselves. None of these accomplishments are insignificant. However, around the age of five, we begin their skill and knowledge training.

There are many options open to parents in this country for how to accomplish this training. Most people automatically assume they will send their children to public schools. This is generally the cheapest and most convenient option. However, it is not without disadvantages. The population of the schools is made of the community at large. The vast majority of the students and teachers in the schools will not hold the same ethical values that you are trying to instill in your child. It means you need to spend a lot of time countering the false notions taught in the schools. Unfortunately, many parents neglect this duty for one reason or another. They assume that they made it through the schools safely, so their children will also. However, public schools are changing over the years. They are not similar to the schools you attended. If you don't want to put the extra effort in to making sure your child has proper ethical training, you should not consider public school as an option.

Private schools are another option. Most of these schools are sponsored by various denominations. They can be costly and hard to get into. Generally, the students attending private schools have higher ethical standards. The teachers try to enforce moral standards. However, you must realize that most denominations are not accurate in their biblical teaching. Your child may be confused when you tell them that God says one thing and their teachers say something else. As with the public schools, you must plan on spending time countering the errors your child may learn in school.

The third option is home schooling. This makes the greatest demands on the parents. It is near impossible for a family to home school unless one parent stays at home to teach the children. The cost is less than private schools, but more than public schools. Since you are the teacher and your own children are the fellow students you can avoid many of the ethical problems of public schools, and avoid the inaccurate Bible teaching.

No matter which option you chose, you will find that your children will begin to develop attachments to people outside of your family. They will deal with school teachers, Bible class teachers, and neighborhood children without you being there. Some parents have difficulties realizing that their children are doing things without their observing what is being done. This must happen. Our goal is to raise godly children to live in this world. They won't always be by our side; we won't always be with them. You will notice that children of this age tend to develop friendships with other children of the same sex. This is normal. The interests of boys and girls differ and children rather associate with people of like interests.

Sibling rivalry is common at this age, especially between children of the opposite sex. Parents will need to take steps to keep the warfare down to friendly skirmishes.

Children of this age period grow steadily. It is not as fast as it has been since birth, nor will it be as fast as in adolescence. Generally, they gain two inches per year.

With their developing independence, they quickly develop their own ideas about what they would like to do. Often these ideas conflict with their parents' desires. Children of this age will sometimes moan and groan about the chores they must do. Not that the chores are taking them away from anything important, but it is not what they wanted to do at the moment. Again, parents must take actions to keep the complaints to a minimum.

It is important that children learn responsibility for their own actions. A parent cannot watch over their children every minute of the day -- nor should a parent want to be watching for the rest of their lives. We are supposed to be training for an independent life. As Christians, each of us is accountable to God for our own actions (Romans 14:12). As parents, you need to teach your child to be accountable for his own actions. A child of this age should be able to take a fairly complex set of instructions and carry them out independently. God holds us responsible for our actions, whether God is standing over us or not (Luke 12:42-46). Children need to learn to be responsible for doing their duties, but it won't come immediately or naturally. There are too many distractions and desirable things in this world that a child must learn to ignore.

To give our children an opportunity to learn responsibility, we must give them the opportunity to fly or to fall. In Luke 19:12-16, notice that the servants who carried out their responsibilities were rewarded beyond their expectation for their good work. Money is a key part of our society and our children need to learn how to handle it responsibly. Give them an allowance after they have learned how to do simple math problems. Allow the child to decide what to spend his money on. You can advise, but the choice must be theirs. Begin to restrict your spending for the child to necessities. If a child sees a new truck that he just has to have or wants a candy bar, tell him he may have it if he has enough money to pay for it out of his own allowance. At first they will buy everything they can, keeping the money on hand to an absolute minimum. If they run out of money, sympathize with them, but DO NOT HELP THEM OUT! Very quickly they will learn that if they want something more than a cheap toy that breaks in a week, they will have to save their allowance.

Set the allowance level low, so they are forced to save to get most items they are interested in purchasing. Do not give them an advance on their next allowance. They need to learn to live within their means. Sometimes, when we are out shopping, one of my children will see something he wishes to purchase, but he had left his money at home. Here, I will buy the item for him, but he must pay me back when we get home. Frequently, the child discovers he didn't have quite as much money as he thought he had. Now, you have two choices, either put up the item until he can get enough money to finish paying you back, or my favorite option is to charge them a 10% fee for the shortfall that comes out of their next allowance.

Allowances can be used in other ways as well. When a child pours a brand-new bottle of shampoo down the drain or takes a carton of ice cream to the utility room, but forgets to put it in the freezer, charge them for your extra costs.

During earlier ages, I told you to only punish willful disobedience or negligence on their part. When a child reaches the middle childhood years, this needs to be expanded. Ignorance on the child's part should no longer be an excuse for not doing something. You may choose to soften the punishment, but a child should be held responsible for learning the rules. See Luke 12:47-48. As adults, we are held responsible for following the laws of our land, whether we learned them or not.

If a child is to learn responsibility, the child must be able to make choices on their own. So give the child an opportunity to choose as frequently as you can. The trick on the parent's part is to make sure that all the choices are things the parent can live with. If the child has fallen into a rut of only eating cereal every morning and you want them to eat something else for variety, offer them a choice of pancakes or eggs and toast. When the child says, "I want cereal!", respond with "that wasn't one of the choices." The child feels a little bit better because it was his choice and you accomplish your goal. As a tip, if there is one choice that you can live with, but you would rather they not pick it, put it first in the list. Most children reject the first choice unless it is something they badly want.

Giving choices is good training for adulthood. While reading through the Scriptures, notice how many choices God gives us in our lives. He even allows us to make the wrong choice at times so that we can learn from our mistakes. Whenever a choice is made, make sure the child stays with the decision. Nothing is more frustrating than a child who constantly changes his mind. When we are at a restaurant, I let the children make their choice for meals, but once the order is place I tell them they cannot change their minds. This has caused a few tears on occasion, but they have learned to be more thoughtful about their selection. If a child makes a bad choice, do not give in and rescue them from their decision. Let them see for themselves that it was a poor choice so they can make better ones in the future.

Encourage personal responsibility for their actions. In Proverbs 9:12, we are told that we will bear the results of our own actions. God punishes us for our own sins (Jeremiah 31:30). It is normal for people to want to blame someone else for their problems. Look at what Adam and Eve did when God confronted them with their sin in Genesis 3:12-13. Children have a natural tendency to blame each other when asked. "Who left the milk out?" "Johnnie had it out last." "I did not! Sue got a drink after me!" Sometimes the children decide it is best not to say anything at all. This can make it difficult as a parent to decide who to punish. In the cases where you can't figure out who the culprit is, admit it to the children and then announce that in this situation everyone will share the punishment. Peer pressure between the children will make sure it doesn't happen frequently. If, after announcing the punishment, someone is suddenly volunteered, then it is likely that everyone knew who the culprit was, but would not say. Thank the children for their honesty, but tell them it was too late this time and administer the punishment.

Sometimes children swing the other way and become tattlers and self-appointed judges. As a parent, you need to teach your children that the parents of the other children decide what is allowable or not. This is the way God treats us (see Romans 14:4). However, make sure that the safety of others is their personal responsibility. If they see another child doing something dangerous, then it is not tattling to get a parent to help. Make it clear to the child that he is not allowed to enforce the rules. Eventually, when they get older and we place them in charge, they will be given some limited authority. But for now, they must live with being the follower, not the leader. Children (and adults too for that matter) have a tough time learning the subtle difference between these two points. However, it is important for them to learn this lesson.

Too often, parents take on too much of the responsibility for their children's actions. If a child doesn't come home for dinner on time, don't go searching for them to make them come to dinner, nor keep a plate warm for them. When they come in after the table has been cleared, tell them they missed out, but there is always breakfast in the morning. If a child forgets to do his homework, though you reminded him to do it before going out to play, then he gets the grade that he earned. Give the children reminders, but do not nag them into doing anything (Proverbs 21:9). As a child gets older, make them responsible for their own bedtime and wake up time. Get them an alarm clock, show them how to set it, and tell them they are on their own. Come morning, when they are exhausted from only getting two hours of sleep last night, they will live with the consequences of their own action.

Learning to be responsible for their own actions give the children the benefit of independent thinking. They will be better able to resist temptation and peer pressure if they know how to decide and weigh the consequences of their actions (I Peter 4:4-5). They will also have a fairer appreciation of their own worth (Galatians 6:3-5). Too often though, we parents do things that prevent our children from learning responsibility. Some parents take a child's responsibility on their own shoulders. For example, when your child comes home with a bad report card, do you say "We have to study harder" or "You need to buckle down"? The former statement implies you hold some responsibility for the bad grade. The later places the responsibility on the student who earned the grade. Some parents try to rescue their children from all harm. When the child fools around and misses their ride to school or some activity, do we drop everything and drive them ourselves? Do you chase after a child's bus when they forgot their homework or lunch? Rescuing a child occasionally is not harmful, but do it too often and it becomes a habit. A child doesn't need to be responsible if they can count on Mom and Dad to fix any problems they may cause. If a child forgets their lunch on a field trip, no harm will come from going without a meal and they will be less likely to walk off without their lunch the next time.

If spanking and other forms of discipline are done well in the earlier years, then the frequency of disciplining your children should decrease as they get older. You will never totally avoid disciplining, even into the teenage years. While spanking will become less favored over other choices of discipline, it should never be ruled out because "The kids are too old." I firmly believe the punishment should fit the offense and there are several offenses where spanking is the most natural form of punishment. Many things that our children do wrongly carry a natural consequence. These consequences can be used as a punishment. However, some things do not. When there are no natural consequences, then spanking should be used to deter further misbehavior. For example, spanking can be used to punish complaining, defiance, rudeness, or tantrums. God holds us accountable for every idle word that we may speak (Matthew 12:36). Children need to be taught not to be careless with their tongues.

When the rod needs to be administered, you need to make the punishment just severe enough that they will not want a repeat. As the child gets older, the switch will need to be a bit bigger and the number of swats may need to be increased. When spanking, give slow, measured licks to the bare bottom. The spacing of the swats makes them more effective and trying to switch through denim jeans will not work.

As a child gets older, you can use the loss of things and privileges that a child considers important as a form of punishment. However, you need to be careful to make sure the child knows the potential loss before the infraction, not afterwards. If you announce the loss of a privilege after the problem occurs, then the punishment comes across as arbitrarily chosen. Think about our Lord. The punishment awaiting all wrong doers is clearly spelled out far in advance. For example, you can tell a child "If your grades don't improve next quarter, TV time will be limited to one hour per day."

Making the consequences of a wrongful action be its own punishment can be entertaining for the parent. I have seen some real cleaver punishments over the years. One parent was having problems with a son and daughter fighting with each other. As punishment, she declared that they would have to do everything together for a whole weekend (except private matters, such as the use of the restrooms -- even then, one would have to wait at the door while the other was occupied). It did not totally solve the problem, but their own animosity for each other served as a strong deterrent when they got a concentrated dose of living with each other.

As we stated before, make sure your expectations of the child's behavior is within the child's capability. Nothing is more frustrating than to be given a goal that you can't possibly hope to achieve. If your child is flunking math, don't tell him he must make an "A" the next quarter. Start easy and work them up to the goal. Tell him that next quarter he must make at least a "C-", once that goal is reach then raise the target a little bit higher.

For a child to learn responsibility, he must be given responsibilities. People living in a house are expected to contribute to the operation of the household. There are many chores available for any child. Even a five-year-old can set the dinner table, if someone will set the plates and silverware in a place where he can reach. Each child can take their own dishes from the table at the end of a meal and help clear the table when everyone is done. Older children can be taught how to load a dishwasher and to put the clean dishes away in their proper places.

Children can help with the laundry. Young children can put their own clothes into their drawers. Every child should learn to put their dirty clothes into the clothes' hamper and not to scatter them on the floor of their room. Make it a rule that if clothes are not in the hamper, they don't get washed. For some kids this can provide some motivation, though I know several boys who won't care. Older children can be taught to fold their own clothes. Later, they can learn to sort clothes, load a washer, and transfer wet clothes to the dryer.

Don't overlook yard work. Most children can rake leaves and grass clippings. If you are into gardening, given an area to each child that is all their own. They can plant and weed their own garden. As they watch their work sprout and develop, they learn the excitement of accomplishing something on their own. Older children can help with shoveling snow, spreading fertilizer, and using a lawnmower with supervision.

If a child is old enough to get out toys for himself, then he is old enough to put them away when he is done with them. Make it a rule that toys left out at the end of the day are lost for a time. If they can't keep track of their own toys, they have too many toys. Return a collected toy as a reward. It will be like a brand new present again. Children can also dust the furniture within their reach. Older children can sweep, mop, and run a vacuum cleaner. Inspect their work before they are don. If it doesn't meet your standards, show them what is wrong and have them repeat the chore.

Caring for pets is another way to learn responsibility for someone else. Make the child responsible for feeding and watering their pets. To ensure proper care, make the child's own meal dependent on their animal being feed. If a child refuses to care for their pet, they should lose the right to retain the animal. Don't assume the responsibility for the child. Older children should learn how to wash and groom their pets.

Remember; our goal is to get our children prepared for living on their own one day. Chores are not ways to get slave labor out of our children. They are opportunities to teach our children how to live on their own one day.

Something to Remember
Larry Christenson

The child who has everything done for him, everything given to him, and nothing required of him is a deprived child.

That's a Home
Fred Toothaker

A home is more than just a house, it's more than roof and walls;
It's more than just a place to rest whenever darkness falls.
A home, you'll find, is more than all the boards, the paint, the glass . . .
It's where you'll find some happiness and blessings come to pass.

A home is more than just a house that's built of brick and stone;
It's more than structure beautiful that man may call his own.
Indeed a home is more than laths where plaster has been spread;
It's where your plans are laid and where the Bible's always read.

A home is where there's living, it's where your dreams come true;
It's where the door is open wide for friends to enter through.
Oh, yes, it's where there's fellowship, where hopes will never cease,
A home is more than just a house . . . it's where your soul's at peace.

Nine to Fifteen-Year-Olds

Teaching Self-control

Around the age of nine to ten (on average), our children begin a dramatic series of changes that take them from childhood to adulthood. The precise ages that these changes begin vary from child to child. The order of the changes also varies by the sex of the child and with each individual child. I will present the typical order of changes, but your child may not change in this order.

The reproductive organs begin to mature beginning at the age of nine on average. Since the changes are internal, most girls do not notice the initial changes. The first indication that something is happening is a rapid growth spurt. All girls grow at an average rate of 1 inch per year, but during adolescent this growth accelerates to 2 inches or more per year. Around the age of 11, pubic hair begins to grow around the genitals and under the arms. Most girls experience their first menstrual period around the age of 13. The start of the monthly period indicates that the reproductive system is fully developed, although the girl's body continues to develop. The breasts begin to form around the age of 11 and come to full shape by the age of 16. These ages are averages. Some girls start earlier and others much later. The vast majority of girls reach puberty between the ages of 8 and 15. If a girl begins to develop before the age of 8 or after the age of 15, it is generally wise to have her checked out by a physician. Early and late development can be an indication of a disease, such as cancer. Generally a daughter will begin to develop at the same age as her mother entered puberty.

Since girls have their growth spurts earlier than boys, it makes them appear to mature sooner than boys, but boys too begin to develop around the age of nine. Though some of their reproductive organs are external, the early changes are so subtle and gradual that most boys do not begin to notice the changes until two years later when they experience their first full erection and ejaculation. This is what leads to the common belief that boys develop two years after girls. The order of change is different from those of a girl. Pubic hair growth around the genitals and under the arms begin to develop around the age of 12. The male growth spurt begins on average around the age of 14. Facial hair begins to grow around the age of 16. Muscular development and the broadening of the shoulders are noticeable around the age of 17. Chest hair begins to grow around the age of 18. Complete maturation does not end until near age 21. A boy can begin puberty as early as age nine or as late as age 16. Earlier or later development is not unheard of, but if your son begins before nine or after 16, it is best to have him examined by a physician to make sure there is no disease involved.

These physical changes are triggered by hormones released by the reproductive organs. Girls release large quantities of estrogens and boys release large quantities of androgens. These sudden increases in hormone levels have other side effects than just physical development. Adolescent children experience large mood swings. A happy child becomes very happy; an angered child becomes very angry; and a depressed child will drown in sorrow. During the rapid growth phase, your well-coordinated child will suddenly become very clumsy. Growth starts from the out extremities (hands and feet) and works it's way inwards. The clumsiness is due to the fact that the limbs are now longer than before. Imagine how you would walk if you put on a pair of shoes two sizes too big. In a very real sense, your adolescent child must learn how to walk all over again.   Boys also experience difficulties due to their sudden muscular development. Something that once took all their effort to hold onto is now easily shattered in their hands. All this growing uses up a lot of energy. Your children's appetites increase dramatically during adolescents, especially the boys. The average adult male consumes about 3000 calories a day. The average adult female consumes about 2400 calories a day. However, the average adolescent boy will consume about 5000 calories a day without gaining fat. The rapid use of energy during growth also contributes to your children's sleepiness. Where before they would get up at the crack of dawn, you will find it hard to drag your adolescent child out of bed before noon.

As your child approaches puberty, you will notice a sudden shyness about their bodies. A four or five-year-old child thinks nothing of running around the house buck naked after a bath. However, as puberty approaches, children suddenly don't want anyone to see them without clothing. A part of this is due to an awakening of sexual desires. The child, at first, has no idea what these desires are; after all, they have never experienced them before. However, these desires contribute to a growing awareness of people of the opposite sex. No longer do girls and boys find each other to be "the enemy."

The sexual development of our child brings a new set of dangers that parents must deal with. Parents are often caught unawares by puberty. As you child progresses through the earlier stages, you and the child fall into a comfortable routine. But puberty requires training in a new area. Suddenly your child has new abilities and desires that he has not developed control over. You must keep in mind the wise words that a person with no self-control is defenseless (Proverbs 25:28). The mood swings due to the hormones means a child must put in extra effort to control his own temperament. A child cannot blame losing his cool on his hormones. They may arise from them, but it just means he must learn to exercise greater control over his emotions. Due to extremes in depression, many teenagers harbor thoughts of suicide. The parent must be watchful, because a child is defenseless at first.

Just as you had to be extremely watchful over a child who is just learning to crawl and to walk, you must be watchful over your children in adolescence. No, there isn't much of a danger of their sticking a finger in a wall outlet, but there is a danger of their experimenting with their sexual desires. Too many parents become use to their child's independence and are too laid back in their approach to adolescents. Just because a child gains the capability to have sex doesn't imply he has gained control over his desires with the ability. It is not an accident that Solomon describes the man, lured by the prostitute, as young (Proverbs 7:6-10,21-23). Given the loose moral standards of our current society, parents need to be even more watchful. The CDC Morbidity and Morality Weekly Report, dated March 24, 1995, reports that 68% of all high school seniors claim to be engaging in sexual intercourse. The 1993 Janus Report on Sexual Behavior states that 19% of all men reported having had sexual intercourse before the age of 14! The percentage rises to 74% of all men reported having had sexual intercourse before the age of 18! Until a child develops control over his own body, the parents must be his conscience.

Adolescent children face heavy peer pressure. Few people, teenagers especially, want to be different from those around them. Solomon warned his son not be enticed to follow the crowd (Proverbs 1:10-19). It is during the adolescent years that drug use, wild clothing, and unusual haircuts begin to appear. The children are trying to define themselves as different from their parents, but the same as the crowd he is associating with. Paul warns Christians to be careful of our associations (Ephesians 5:11-12; I Corinthians 15:33). Good friends can encourage a person to be better, but wicked friends can much more easily persuade a person to do wrong.

In September, 2004, Pediatrics published a study linking viewing television programs containing sexual content with teenage sexual activity. Those watching programs that either displayed sexual activity or merely discussed sexual activity where encouraged to engage in sexual activity. The study found that the ten percent who watched the most television with sexual content were twice as likely to engage in sexual intercourse in one year than the ten percent watching the least television with sexual content. As Paul warned, "Evil company corrupts good habits" (I Corinthians 15:33).

Obviously, parents have a full workload laid out for them when it comes to raising teenagers. The most important lesson to teach is self-control. Among Peter's list of characteristics that every Christian is to develop is self-control (II Peter 1:5-7). It is a problem that every Christian must face. Even the apostle Paul spoke of the struggle he had to maintain control over his own body (I Corinthians 9:24-27). We need teach our children how to control their anger (James 1:19-21). We need to instruct our children how to keep a reign over our tongue (James 3:2). Children need to develop the ability to not rial against a false accusation (Matthew 27:11-14). While Saul is not the greatest example in the Bible, he could endure taunts (I Samuel 10:27).

Parents should also teach their children self-control in their spending habits. A child who gets anything he wants will find himself in financial difficulties when he reaches adulthood. Every person has a limited income and each person must exercise restraint to live within that income. A clever way to teach your child money management is to put them in charge of a portion of the household's budget. Pick an area that your child has a strong interest, such as the family's entertainment. Give the child a fixed amount of funds and then ask them to spend it wisely to benefit the family as a whole. For example, suppose you figure that you spend $50 per month on entertainment (movies, rentals, dining, etc.). You give your child $50 at the beginning of each month and tell them this is all they have to entertain the family. They can spend it as they see fit, but it needs to make the family happy or he will be "fired" from his position. Hence, your child learns that money is limited, that things have a cost, that current wants must be balanced with future needs, and that he must think about other people and not his own desires.

Even more obviously, if we are to teach self-control to our children, then we must have control over ourselves. Self-control is learned from God. God teaches us to live properly in this world (Titus 2:11-12). It is a by-product produced when we strive to live the Christian life (Galatians 5:19). David refrained from striking Saul, who was seeking to end his life, because of his strong desire to do God's will (I Samuel 24).

Our teenagers need to learn how to avoid temptation (I Thessalonians 5:22). Satan will always put us into tempting situations, but teenagers need to learn how to recognize those situations. For example, you should have a house rule that they should not have guests of the opposite sex over at your house when the parents are not around. Similarly, teenagers should not visit a friend of the opposite sex if the friend's parents are not at home. If your teenager asks, "Don't you trust me?" The answer is quite simple, "No. You don't have the experience to resist Satan on your own." Did you know that 60% of all teenage sexual activity happens at home?

Your children also need instruction on the influence of their friends. If you asked, most kids think that they are completely independent. However, their idea of independence is separation from their parents. They remain very dependent on their peers. Teenagers need to see this situation clearly, so they can realize where the pressures for immoral behavior are coming from.

Being a faithful Christian is not just the ability to avoid sinful behavior. A Christian must fill their life with so much righteousness that there is no room for sinful activity (Romans 13:14). Keep your teenagers busy doing righteous things. Idleness gives Satan an opportunity to try to get his hooks into your child's soul.

By the time a child has reached adolescence, they usually realize they need to be obedient to the Lord. They have become aware of their own inadequacies in facing temptation. They see the need for help that can only come from the Lord. Paul said he could do all things through Christ, who gives him strength (Philippians 4:13). But help only comes when we join our lives with God's life. There is a mighty battle taking place between God and Satan. It is so big that there are no side lines where we can watch as independent observers. The war is taking place all around us. If we fight independently, the enemy is so great that we will soon be overwhelmed. Yet we can join God's side and have his aid, but we must first make the choice. Will you be on the Lord's side?

Mary Had a Little Boy

Mary had a little boy, his soul was white as snow;
>He never went to Sunday School, 'cause Mary wouldn't go.
He never heard the truth of Christ that thrilled the childish mind;
>While other children went to class, this child was left behind.
And as he grew from babe to youth, she saw to her dismay,
>A soul that once was snowy white became a dingy gray.
Realizing he was lost she tried to win him back,
>But now the soul that once was white had turned an ugly black.
She even started back to church and Bible study too.
>She begged the preacher, "Isn't there a thing that you can do?"
The preacher tried — failed and said, "We're just too far behind.
>I tried to tell you years ago, but you would pay no mind."
And so another soul is lost, that once was white as snow.
>Sunday School could have helped, but Mary wouldn't go.

Author Unknown

When to Have That Little Talk

It is a mixed blessing when our children reach puberty. Our children are growing up. They are moving on to adulthood, leaving childhood behind. Soon all we will have left are memories and a few photographs. There are many dangers that our children must face, which require parents to teach about -- well, shall we say -- delicate subjects. Let's face it, I have a hard enough time talking about sex with my dear wife. The thoughts of instructing my own children is less than appealing. Yet, if I don't do it, who will?

Puberty is the time when our children develop reproductive capabilities. They are experiencing desires that they cannot describe because they never felt them before. Their bodies are rapidly changing from child to adult form. The very changes are often awkward to handle. And everyone wonders, "Is this normal?" The common parental response is to avoid the topic as long as possible. Why embarrass yourself any sooner than you need to? But if we teach our children as they experience these changes, we can give them peace of mind. More importantly, we can guide them to follow the proper path to adulthood. Perhaps they can avoid the pitfalls that many of us took in our ignorance.

God certainly did not leave us in the dark about our sexuality. There is a wealth of information throughout the Scriptures on a wide variety of issues. The details of what needs to be discussed with your child, I have put in a separate book, titled "Growing Up in the Lord."

However, one question that I have been asked is "When is a good time to start discussing these things with my child?" Most parents recognize that we don't want to start too soon. Small children have no concept of sexual relations and don't need such a concept to function in this world. However, if we wait too long, our child might be caught off-guard in an embarrassing or possibly dangerous situation.

When children are small, there is a natural curiosity about where they come from. Usually, a general answer is enough to satisfy their curiosity. For example, babies grow inside a special place in the mother's tummy. When the baby is old enough to live on its own, it is born. If they want to know how the baby got into the mother, explain that babies start when a father and a mother decide to have a baby. A seed from the father joins with a seed from the mother to form the baby. This is usually enough for most children.

Sometime shortly before puberty, children suddenly become aware of their bodies. They become shy about letting anyone see themselves without clothing. This is a normal part of growing up. You may notice that some children become a bit chubby again. It is almost as if they are putting on baby fat again. This is the body's preparation for growth. Growing takes a lot of energy and a child's body will store up fat to supply some of that energy. About this time, it is good to mention that they will shortly be changing from a childhood to adulthood. These changes will include a lot of body changes. For both boys and girls, mention that one of the changes is a rapid change in the size of their bodies. While the growth happens, they will sometimes get clumsy as they readjust to their new size.

For girls, moms should talk to the girls about periods. Talk about the monthly blood flows and instruct them on how to wear a sanitary napkin. It would also be good to have them carry one with them, since you never know when the first period will take place. This may bring up other questions, which you can address. If a question doesn't come up that you know you need to talk about during adolescence, save it for later. Make sure your daughter understands to let you know when her period has started. Once it has, plan on taking some private time when you can go into details about the responsibilities of being an adult and the additional desires and temptations your daughter will be facing.

For boys, dads should talk to their boys about erections and wet dreams. These are usually the first indication a boy notices that they have entered puberty. Both body functions can be embarrassing when they happen. Tell your boys to let you know when these events happen and you will teach them about the responsibilities of being an adult, the new desires they will have, and the additional temptations they will be facing. Talking about growing up will probably bring up other questions that your son has been wondering about. Answer each one as simply and as openly as you can, but don't be surprise if some of the things you know you need to talk about does not come up. Save these topics for when your son has started growing and can understand sexual desire first hand.

After your child has gained the ability to have sex, make sure you have a detailed talk with your child about sexual desires, the need for controlling those desires, and the dangers of Satan's temptations before they begin dating. In this corrupt time, you should also discuss the sin of homosexuality shortly after your child has entered adolescence. Many corrupt people know that children are easy targets for perverse sexual practices during early adolescence. They take advantage of the new desires in teenagers, who do not have experience, to lead them into sin.

Sixteen to Nineteen-Year-Olds

Teaching Independence

After all the hard work that you put into raising godly children, now is the time to reap some benefits of that work. Your older teenagers are still living at home, but we now must prepare them for eventually living on their own. Soon the time will come when they must leave Mom and Dad and cleave to their spouse (Genesis 2:24). After having them under your feet for nearly 20 years, it is hard to think about them being gone. It is also difficult for them. All they have known is life with their family. Therefore, in the later teenage years, we must get our children ready to live independently.

The parent's role shifts from director of a child's life to an advisor. They still live at home and the parent is always available for guidance, but the child must now make his own decisions. And one of the hardest lessons to learn is when to ask for help. It is so tempting to jump right in and show the child what he must do. Nevertheless, he needs to learn how to handle mistakes when Mom and Dad are there to given him support and encouragement. If you don't give him the opportunity to fail, he will have a rough time adapting to independent living.

Older teenagers should be encouraged to earn their own spending money. If you have been giving the child an allowance, forewarn them that when they reach the age of 16, you will no longer be supplying them spending cash. Gradually get them responsible for their expenses. For example, driving is a privilege, not a right. Tell the child he will be allowed to drive if he pays for the insurance increase, license fees, and the gas he uses in the family car. The insurance payment not only gives a child fiscal responsibility, but it also provides motivation to a child to keep his driving record clean. If he is a careless driver, he may soon find out that he can't afford to drive. Don't supply a teenager with his own car. If he wants his own set of wheels, he must pay for it himself. Only co-sign a teenager's car loan if he understands that if he misses a payment, you get to keep the car that month. If possible, encourage your child to pay for their first car in full without a loan. Saving in advance for large purchases is a good habit that few people are taught these days.

Break your teenager into financial responsibility in their mid-teenage years by giving them a clothing allowance equivalent to what you have been spending on their clothing. From this allowance, they will be expected to buy their own clothing and toiletries. Set the allowance just high enough that they can afford decent clothes, but not so high that they can purchase expensive clothing items. If the child just has to have this one particular dress or these really important shoes, tell them to either save the money or earn the money on their own. A teenager should be responsible for all of his clothing purchases, even his socks and underwear. By the time a child has his own job, you should wean him from the clothing allowance. He should be totally responsible for all of his purchases. Suddenly, getting a new shirt for his birthday will be a valued gift.

Attendance at college should also be treated as a privilege and not a right. Every parent should encourage their children to attend college, but a college degree is not essential to earn a living in this world. It makes things easier and gives you a higher starting position and salary, but a person can reach the same point with a lot of hard work instead of an education. The goal is to get the child to see the value of an education so they will appreciate it and put effort into obtaining their degree. Your family may decide to help pay for some costs of an education as an additional encouragement. For example, you may offer to pay the college fees, books, or room and board. However, I strongly suggest that you do not supply any spending money. The child earns money to pay for his expenses. There are multiple ways for a person to put themselves through college without incurring a large debt. School schedules allow a dedicated person to work part-time or even full-time while attending classes. Many schools have cooperative programs where a student alternates working at a company in his chosen field with semesters at college. A student can often earn enough money cooping to support themselves during the work semester and pay their college expenses during the following school semester. The armed services offer ROTC programs where they will pay a child's college expenses in exchange for a few years in the service. Check into grants and scholarships to decrease the costs of college. As a last resort, a child can also get a student loan to meet their college expenses. I generally discourage this last option, because it is easy to rack up a huge debt in a short while. It is hard enough starting out on your own. Most young people don't need to be worrying about making payments on a college loan.

A college education is more valued when a person can translate the cost of an education into actual hours that must be worked. Too many people treat advanced education lightly. They end up not appreciating what they have and do not put enough effort into it. In addition, working for your own education reduces the amount of idle time a young person has and will tend to keep him out of trouble.

Similarly, once a child is out of school, they should begin to pay rent while they are living at home. It seems awkward to charge your own child for the privilege of living with you. However, a child needs to be encouraged to become independent and some children will stay around longer than they should if they are given a free ride.

The chores that an older teenager is given should also prepare him for independent living. An older child should have complete responsibility for his own laundry, especially before going off to college. Make him responsible for some meals. For example, make him prepare all his own breakfast and lunches, or require that he make dinner periodically. Send your older child to the store periodically to buy food for the family. Make sure he knows how to find bargains and how to use coupons. One way to encourage frugal shopping habits is to estimate how much it will cost you to buy your usual purchases and give this amount to your child. Tell him he can keep the change for any additional savings he comes up with.

If an older teenager is going to live on his own, he will have to learn how to handle additional freedom, for freedom is accompanied by responsibility. Allow your child to set his own schedule and his own bedtimes. At first he may abuse the privilege, but a few blurry eyed days at school will soon cause him to value his sleep. When your child is out on a date, insist on knowing who they are going out with and where they plan to be in case an emergency comes up. Also insist on knowing when they plan to be home. Tell them that if they don't make it by their chosen time, you will assume they had a problem and you will come looking for them. Moms, if you are bold and really want to cure them of tardiness, show up on the doorstep of their friend's house in curlers and a housecoat over your street clothes. You may look like a sight, but your teenager will "die" having his mother seen in public in such a state. While he is turning beet-red, simply remind him that he didn't make his own appointment and you wanted to make sure he was all right. Saying this in front of his friends will drive the point home.

Make sure that the opportunities for temptation are limited. Be blunt with your child if you think that a chosen destination is dangerous spiritually. Just because your teenager has the body of an adult doesn't mean he has the experiences of an adult in recognizing bad situations.

Similarly, maintain a strict code of behavior on your children while they live with you. Insist that there will be no drinking, no drugs, no smoking, no foul language, no sexual play while they live under your roof. Severe violations of your house rules should result in a loss of home privilege. If they cannot restrain themselves while living in your home, then they can find their own place. Make sure they understand they are welcome to return when they repent of their wicked ways and they are willing to abide by your rules.

Build Me a Son, O Lord

Build me a son, O Lord, who will be strong enough to know when he is weak, and brave enough to face himself when he is afraid. One who will be proud and unbending in defeat, but humble and gentle in victory.

A son whose wishbone will not be where his backbone should be; a son who will know that to know himself is the foundation stone of knowledge.

Rear him, I pray, not in the paths of ease and comfort but under the stress and spur of difficulties and challenges. Here let him learn to stand up in the storm; here let him learn compassion for those who fail.

Build me a son whose heart will be clean, whose goal will be high. A son who will master himself before he seeks to master other men. One who will learn to laugh, yet never forget how to weep. One who will reach into the future, yet never forget the past.

And after all these are his, add I pray, enough of a sense of humor so that he may always be serious, yet never take himself too seriously; a touch of humility, so that he may always remember the simplicity of true greatness; the open mind of true wisdom; the meekness of true strength.

Then, I, his father, will dare to whisper, I have not lived in vain.

General Douglas MacArthur

45

The Problem Child

Some of you, after reading this far into this book, are thinking: "This is all fine and good, but I wish someone told me this years ago." What do you do if you started out your child rearing on the wrong foot?

Others of you are dealing with difficult children, the ones generally labeled as "attention deficit disorder (ADD)," "attention deficit hyperactive disorder (ADHD)," or "oppositional defiant disorder (ODD)." Every child is different, but some seem to be wired to get into trouble constantly. Unfortunately, our society has a fascination with drugs to cure all ailments. As a society, we have a strong tendency to over prescribe drugs. While drugs might help alleviate the symptoms, they do not deal with the problems. Too often, the drugs dampen a child's thought processes to the point that they appear to be well-behaved because they are too spaced out on the drug. Many parents discover they have a problem on their hands when the drug wears off. The child behaves as bad or even worse than before because they rarely are given an opportunity to deal with their problems.

First, understand that things will not improve if you continue using the wrong methods. It is likely that you will not be able to completely repair all the previous damage that you may have inadvertently caused in your child's younger years. However, ignoring the problem and continuing your present course will not improve the matter. Sit down with your child and explain that you have been learning about parenting from God's Word and that you have discovered that you had been doing some things incorrectly. Apologize for the error and explain that you will be changing how you handle things in the future. Some aspects of the changes they may not like, but assure them that God said this is a better way. If your child is old enough, sit down with them and have a family Bible study on the topic of raising children. Not only will this warn them of the upcoming changes that you plan to make, it also helps them to understand God's Word so they will not make the same mistakes you made when they become parents.

Second, you have a lot of lost ground to make up. It will not be easy and it will not come quickly. Where a forewarned parent has a number of years to adjust and tailor their child's training as the child is growing, you will have fewer years to get the same lessons accomplished. If you are starting with a teenager, you will not be able to concentrate on teaching self-control. You will have to also teach the lessons on obedience and responsibility that the child had missed. The concentrated lessons will not be enjoyable for you or the child, but they are necessary.

Third, no method works if it is followed in a hit-and-miss manner. There must be consistency in application. This is especially true with ADD, ADHD, and ODD children. It is very exasperating to correct a child only to find him immediately repeating that for which you just punished him. Parents facing this often start trying a variety of things in hopes of finding one that works. Ultimately they throw up their hands in disgust deciding that nothing works, so why bother. But here the parents are their own worse enemy. Most children with ADD, ADHD, or ODD thrive on consistency. Their thought processes are easily distracted and they often make rash choices without fully thinking about the results. A consistent approach gives them an anchor to hold onto in the storms of their thoughts. So long as the punishments for incorrect behavior are just, fair, and consistent, discipline for such children is a form of comfort.

This is why children with ADD, ADHD, and ODD thrive on disciplined sports, such as martial arts. The rules for behavior are spelled out; Misbehavior is disciplined; and the activity gives the children an outlet for their energy.

Once in a while, a child will go astray despite our best efforts. It seems that most people I have met with wayward children feel they have done everything possible, but the child chose to stray. We are all free-agents, able to chose to obey or disobey our Lord. However, there are few families that I have met where it wasn't apparent that they had not been following God's teachings on raising children as closely as they should have been. The Bible lists a number of godly men who were unable to raise godly children. Eli, the High Priest of the Most High, raised wicked sons. The reason for his failure is clearly stated: he never restrained them (I Samuel 3:12-13). Like many modern philosophers, Eli did not punish his children for wrong doing, but let them do as they will. Sometimes, children raised without proper discipline grow up to be godly people, but it is despite their parent's instructions, not because of it. King David had a number of rebellious sons. In I Kings 1:5-6, Adonijah's rebellion was attributed to the fact that David always tried to please his children. We can't always be a chum with our children and raise them to be respectful and obedient. Children need correction. It is a part of their training.

Often, parents who raised their children with poor technique face their biggest challenge when their children reach their teenage years. The seemingly tranquil child now asserts his independence, but instead of moving towards godliness, he chases after the wicked. What is a parent to do?

Spanking: There is nothing in the Scriptures to indicate that spanking must be limited to young children. Many times you can find effective, non-spanking forms of discipline for older children. However, there are times when nothing better drives the point home than a simple spanking. Consider spanking as an option when you are dealing with willful rebellion, backtalk, or foul-language.

Restricted Privileges: Parents and children both assume that everything that comes their way is theirs by right. Few people learn to appreciate that most of the things that we take for granted are privileges. If this lesson would only sink into more people we would have fewer problems with pride. Sometimes a point is made by removing privileges of going places or engaging in certain entertainment activities. If you chose to punish by removing driving privileges or limiting television viewing, you must make sure that the consequences are spelled out before the violation occurs. Older children need to be able to weigh the temptation against the consequences. It makes the punishment much more effective.

The removal of privileges can be an effective tool in correcting access to things that help a child accomplish their wrongful practices. Is your son's rebelliousness coming from associating with wicked friends? Then limit his free time in the evenings and weekends. Not only forbid him from leaving home for a period of time, but also make sure that his extra time is filled with special chores to be accomplished. Have you discovered that your daughter is experimenting with drugs? Then remove those things that allow her to purchase the drugs. Eliminate her allowance and require her to earn her own spending money. Severely restrict her telephone privileges. I am surprised how many parents, who told me their child was into drugs also told me that their children had their own phone -- paid for by the parents! Why make it easy for them to arrange drug deals? Yes, I understand that phones do not lead to drug use, but if you know a child is into drugs, these same tools can facilitate the purchase of drugs. Accomplish two things at once. Punish the child by removing a privilege and have the lost privilege cause the child extra difficulty in violating your rules.

In the extreme, a child can lose access to all luxury. If you find drugs hidden in your child's room, then make it difficult to hid drugs in the room. Remove every luxury from the room, and I do mean everything that is not an absolute necessity. Remove all the furniture, except a mattress. Remove all the posters, pictures, trophies, games, and collectibles. Reduce the clothing down to the minimum needed to get by, such as two sets of everyday clothing and one better outfit for Sunday. Sell or give away all the items. Make it clear to the child that these privileges may be earned back by extended good behavior. This probably sounds extreme, but some offenses require extreme action to show the significance of sinful behavior.

Withdrawal: Some sins can be effectively punished by removing access to the encouragement of the family. Just as an unrepentant sinner can be made to see the repugnancy of sin by the withdrawal of the congregation, the same lesson can be used on a smaller scale within the family. Parents commonly used this method with their younger children without thinking about what is being accomplished. We often send our children to their rooms for periods of time when they misbehave. The isolation gives them time to cool down and think about what they have done. They soon realize the separation from the rest of the family is boring. Too many games require someone to play with. This form of discipline is effective for children who are fighting or throwing tantrums.

When an older teenager constantly rebels, refusing to obey the rules of the home, it may be necessary to remove him from the home. Just as a sin left in a congregation can spread rapidly to all the members, a rebellious child's behavior can influence younger children to sin in their own ways as they grow up. Pack the rebellious child's bags and put them on the porch. Few things make a bigger impact than to come home and find you are no longer welcomed. Offer to help him find a place to rent. You may even offer to pay the first few months rent, so he can find a job to support himself. Make sure that he understands he is welcomed to return if he will repent of his sins and is willing to live by your rules. Just because the child is out of your home, it does not relieve you of your responsibilities to try to bring him out of his sins. His removal from your home is to make him understand your disapproval and your seriousness in not tolerating wrong doing. It also is important to keep his sin from spreading to your other children. They will learn that sin has a serious consequence when they observe your actions.

Punishing a child is usually difficult on a parent. We want the best for our children and it is difficult to inflict discomfort and pain on our little ones. It becomes even more difficult when a child forces us to use extreme measures. Not only does it distresses us to see our child in trouble, but the fact we have to take these steps makes us realize that we haven't done our part as parents. We have failed our child, ourselves, and our Lord. However, as with any sin, feeling sorry for ourselves is not going to correct the situation. Every sin has a consequence and if we haven't lived up to the Lord's rules for raising godly children, then we need to accept the consequences and do the best we can to fix the problem we have caused. Even parents have to learn to accept the responsibility for their own mistakes.

Why Do You Act Like That?
Terrence D. McLean

When four-year-old Johnny went to the grocery store with his mommy, Johnny snitched a piece of candy from the bottom shelf and promptly ate it. His mother saw him do it and she took the candy wrapper and hid it behind some cans of beans.

When Johnny was six, he was in the front seat of the car when his daddy was pulled over by a policeman. When his dad gave the officer his driver's license, he also slipped the policeman a twenty dollar bill. When the cop would not take the money, Johnny's dad cussed him out.

When eight-year-old Johnny went to a family reunion picnic, he roasted marshmallows with the other kids while the grown-ups told funny stories about how they had cheated on their taxes over the years.

When Johnny was ten-years-old, he went hunting with his grandpa. They helped each other get through the barbed wire fence and grandpa tore down the "no-trespassing" sign and hid it under some fallen branches.

When twelve-year-old Johnny spent the weekend with his aunt and uncle, Johnny fell and broke his glasses. His aunt called the insurance company and told them that Johnny's glasses had been stolen from their care, and she collected $115.

When Johnny was thirteen, he mad first string on the Junior High football team. Johnny played right guard, and the coach taught Johnny how to block. He also taught Johnny how to grab the opponent by the shirt in a way that the officials could not see.

When Johnny turned fifteen, he got his first summer job, working at a produce stand on a busy road. The manager taught Johnny how to put the overripe tomatoes in the bottom of the carton and how to set the scale so that it added a couple of ounces to every purchase.

When sixteen-year-old Johnny was sent to the store to pick up some things, his dad told him to pick up some beer while he was out. To make that easier, Johnny's dad fixed him up with some phoney ID, just in case.

When Johnny was seventeen and a senior, he found chemistry class to be ver difficult and he was failing. His class president, however, sold Johnny the answers to the chemistry test.

It was near midnight when the phone rang at the home of Johnny's mom and dad. His mom answered the call.

"Ma'am," a husky voice said, "we have your son here at the county jail."

After about ninety days of legalities and lawyers fees, Johnny was on probation for grand theft and was attending weekly meetings of Narcotics Anonymous.

"How could you do this to your mom and me?" his father shouted. And his mom chimed in with "Where did you learn to act like that?" His aunt said, "If there is one thing I can't stand, it's a kid that lies." "John," said his grandpa, "we must all obey the law."

Train up a child in the way he should go: and when he is old, he will not depart from it.   Proverbs 22:6

www.ingramcontent.com/pod-product-compliance
Lightning Source LLC
Chambersburg PA
CBHW021116020426
42331CB00004B/517